SUPER
SURPRISING
TRIVIA
ABOUT
the
UNEXPLAINED

by Megan Cooley Peterson

CAPSTONE PRESS
a capstone imprint

Spark is published by Capstone Press, an imprint of Capstone
1710 Roe Crest Drive, North Mankato, Minnesota 56003
capstonepub.com

Copyright © 2024 by Capstone. All rights reserved. No part of this
publication may be reproduced in whole or in part, or stored in a retrieval
system, or transmitted in any form or by any means, electronic, mechanical,
photocopying, recording, or otherwise, without written permission of the
publisher.

Library of Congress Cataloging-in-Publication Data
Names: Peterson, Megan Cooley, author.
Title: Super surprising trivia about the unexplained / by Megan Cooley
Peterson.
Description: North Mankato, Curiosities and wonders. : Capstone
Press, 2023. | Series: Super surprising trivia you can't resist | Includes
bibliographical references and index. | Audience: Ages 9-11 | Audience:
Grades 4-6 | Summary: "Think you know a lot about all things strange,
mysterious, and disturbing? Get ready to learn even more! From the lost city
of Atlantis to famous missing people to the possible existence of Bigfoot, get
ready to learn all about the world's strange and mysterious happenings that
have baffled experts for years"— Provided by publisher.
Identifiers: LCCN 2023000913 (print) | LCCN 2023000914 (ebook) |
ISBN 9781669050414 (hardcover) | ISBN 9781669071778 (paperback) |
ISBN 9781669050377 (pdf) | ISBN 9781669050391 (kindle edition) |
ISBN 9781669050407 (epub)
Subjects: LCSH: Curiosities and wonders—Juvenile literature.
Classification: LCC AG244 .P48 2023 (print) | LCC AG244 (ebook) | DDC
031.02—dc23/eng/20230112
LC record available at https://lccn.loc.gov/2023000913
LC ebook record available at https://lccn.loc.gov/2023000914

Editorial Credits
Editor: Mandy Robbins; Designer: Heidi Thompson; Media Researcher:
Jo Miller; Production Specialist: Tori Abraham

Image Credits
Alamy: Ian Dagnall, 18, World History Archive, 17, Barry Iverson, 19,
Chroma Collection, 21, Dennis Cox, 16, Heritage Image Partnership Ltd,
8 (bottom), PA Images, 23; Getty Images: Bettmann, 24, ROGER HARRIS/
SCIENCE PHOTO LIBRARY, 15, VICTOR HABBICK VISIONS, 6; Science
Source: Jaime Chirinos, 26 (bottom); Shutterstock: Aksara.k, 27, Ammit Jack,
13, Daniel Eskridge, 25 (both), 28, 29, Everett Collection, 20, Guenter Albers,
Cover (bottom right), Hollygraphic, (design element) throughout, Jay
Ondreicka, 12, Lubomira08, 26 (top), mexrix, (background) throughout,
Peter Stuckings, 11, Philippe Clement, 22, Raggedstone, 4, 5, Rockweiler,
8 (top), seawhisper, Cover (top left), 9, Stockbym, 14, Vac1, Cover (bottom
left), Vicky Jirayu, Cover (top right), WindVector, 7

All internet sites appearing in back matter were available and accurate when
this book was sent to press.

Printed and bound in China. P05379

TABLE OF CONTENTS

Words in **bold** are in the glossary.

The WORLD of the UNEXPLAINED

Secrets lie in every corner of the world. People disappear. Mummies are found. Strange creatures are spotted. What will you discover in the world of the unexplained?

WHAT Is this PLACE?

The Bermuda Triangle is an area in the Atlantic Ocean. More than 50 ships and 20 planes have disappeared there.

Manitowoc

Ludington

WISCONSIN

MICHIGAN

Milwaukee

Benton Harbor

Chicago

ILLINOIS

INDIANA

People go missing in the Lake Michigan Triangle too. Steven Kubacki disappeared there in 1978. After 15 months, he showed up 700 miles away. He didn't remember where he had been.

Stonehenge was built between 3000 and 1520 **BCE**. Who built this circle of 100 large stones? No one knows.

A **crop circle** popped up near Stonehenge in 1996. It appeared in less than an hour during the day.

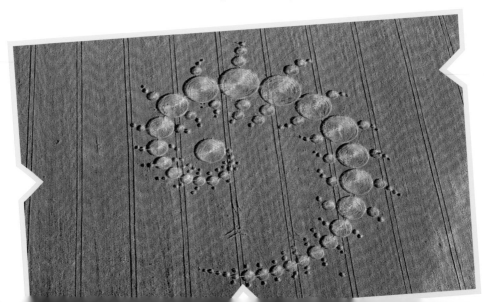

The trees in Poland's Crooked Forest

grow at right angles. Nobody knows why.

It took 2.3 million giant stones to build the Great Pyramid. Each one weighed at least 2 tons. Perhaps workers used ramps.

More than 2,100 giant stone jars dot the Plain of Jars in Laos. The jars are heavy. Each one weighs several tons. The jars were used to bury the dead. But who made them?

A flame burns behind the Eternal Flame Falls in New York. Underground gases feed it. Scientists aren't sure how the gases reach the flame.

It rained meat in Kentucky in 1876.

It may have been vulture vomit.

Legends say Atlantis sank into the ocean in 9600 BCE. People still search for this lost city.

An **asteroid** hit Earth 65 million years ago. All non-bird dinosaurs died. It's unknown why birdlike dinosaurs lived.

MYSTERIOUS MUMMIES

Xin Zhui's mummy is the most well-**preserved** one ever found. She died almost 2,200 years ago in China. An unknown liquid kept her body fresh.

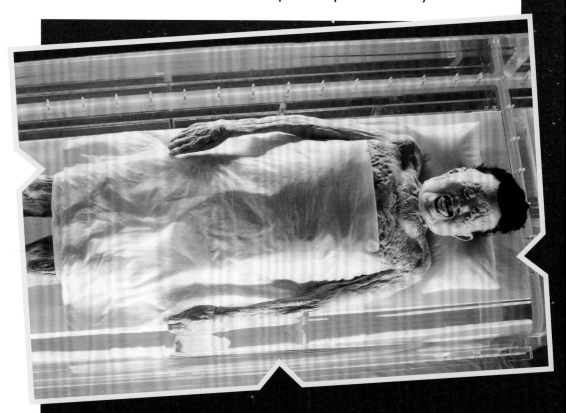

In 1838, a British explorer found Pharaoh Menkaure's coffin. He shipped it to a British museum. But the ship sank on its way there. People still search for it.

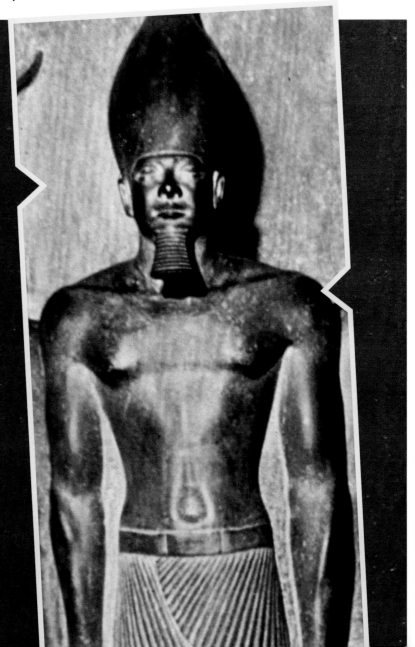

Almost 1,000 **bog** mummies have been dug up in Europe. Many appear to have been killed.

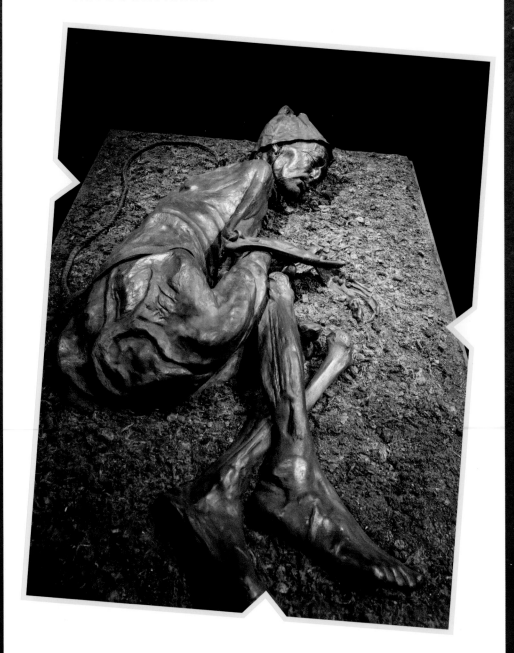

King Tut's mummy had a broken leg. Some believe the Egyptian king was sick. Others say he was killed.

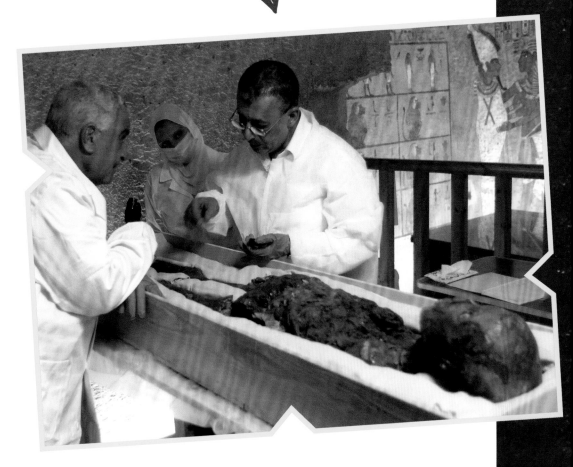

A "screaming" mummy was uncovered in Egypt in 1881. His face was twisted in pain.

MISSING!

American pilot Amelia Earhart disappeared over the Pacific in 1937. No one has found her or her plane.

George Mallory disappeared climbing Mount Everest in 1924. Climbers found his body in 1999. His camera remains missing.

The Peking man **fossils** belonged to an **ancient** human. China sent them to the United States in 1941. But they were lost on the way.

The Jules Rimet World Cup soccer trophy was stolen in 1966. It was found six days later. In 1983, it was stolen again. It's still missing.

Are these CREATURES REAL?

Bigfoot may have been caught on film in 1967. A home movie showed a hairy, apelike beast. It walked near trees.

Yetis are said to live in the Himalayan mountains. They look like Bigfoot but white. Some stand up to 10 feet tall.

The doglike chupacabra is said to drink the blood of animals.

The Loch Ness Monster may swim in Scotland. Stories say "Nessie" has a long body and a snakelike head.

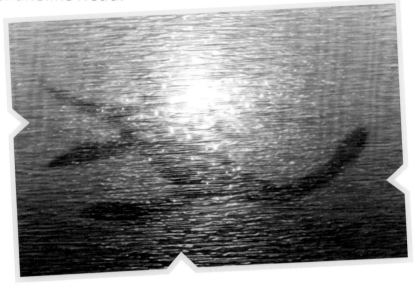

Mongolian death worms are said to grow up to 5 feet long.

Watch out for kappa near Japanese rivers.

These froglike creatures may eat children!

Stories say the Jersey Devil haunts New Jersey. It has red eyes, leathery wings, and horns.

Scotland's Big Gray Man stands up to 20 feet tall.

People say it lives high in the mountains.

In 1966, the Mothman flew beside a speeding car.

The passengers said it had red eyes and huge wings.

Glossary

ancient (AYN-shunt)—from a long time ago

asteroid (AS-tuh-royd)—a large rock that travels through space

BCE (bee-cee-EE)—before the year zero; stands for "before the common era"

bog (BOG)—a type of wetland that includes wet, spongy ground and pools of muddy water

crop circle (KROP cir-kuhl)—a circular pattern of flattened stalks in a field of grain

fossil (FAH-suhl)—the remains or traces of plants, animals, and people that are preserved as rock

legend (LEJ-uhnd)—a story passed down through the years that may not be completely true

preserve (pri-ZURV)—to keep something fresh

Read More

Harder, Megan. *Inside the Bermuda Triangle.* Minneapolis: Lerner Publications, 2023.

Harper, Benjamin. *The Secret Life of the Loch Ness Monster*. North Mankato, MN: Capstone Press, 2023.

Storm, Marysa. *Crop Circles*. Mankato, MN: Black Rabbit Books, 2022.

Internet Sites

170 Fun Facts for Kids
kidpillar.com/fun-facts-for-kids-weird-but-true/

Bermuda Triangle Facts & Worksheets
kidskonnect.com/geography/bermuda-triangle/

Mummy Mystery: King Tut
kids.nationalgeographic.com/history/article/king-tut

Index

About the Author

Megan Cooley Peterson is a children's book author and editor. Her book *How To Build Hair-Raising Haunted Houses* (Capstone Press, 2011) was selected as a Book of Note by the TriState Young Adult Review Committee. When not writing, Megan enjoys movies, books, and all things Halloween. She lives in Minnesota with her husband and daughter.